Kid Contraptions

by Robynne Eagan

illustrated by Teresa Mathis

Teaching & Learning Company

1204 Buchanan St., P.O. Box 10
Carthage, IL 62321

The activity demonstrated on the front cover is the
Thread Spool, Box and String Crane (page 21).

Cover by Girard Photography

Copyright © 1995, Teaching & Learning Company

ISBN No. 1-57310-023-4

Printing No. 987654321

Teaching & Learning Company
1204 Buchanan St., P.O. Box 10
Carthage, IL 62321

This book belongs to

_____

Foreword

Kid Contraptions offers an exciting cross-curriculum approach to design and technology. This unique collection of do-it-yourself projects is geared to develop essential creative problem-solving skills by leading children to discoveries. Turn your space into an invention lab and watch children learn as they turn everyday items into original kid contraptions that really work.

Acknowledgements

A special thank you to the children who have shared their creative genius with me, especially Kiersten Eagan who shared her Just for Fun Inventions. For technical assistance, guidance, editing and enthusiasm, thank you to Peter Hunter (P.Eng.) and Charles Eagan (App. Math, E. Eng.). Special appreciation to the teachers and students of St. James School, Colgan and McNab Public School, Renfrew County who have shared their ideas and thought inventively with me. And finally, I would like to acknowledge the creative thinkers, all through time, who have approached life from a different angle and shared in the excitement of contraptions for the sheer joy of it.

Table of Contents

Dear Teacher or Parent,

Turn everyday items into exciting kid contraptions and watch active learning in progress!

Tap into a child's natural fascination, curiosity and enthusiasm to make design and technology appealing and accessible to primary children. *Kid Contraptions* provides active learning projects geared to help children better understand the world in which they live. Process and content are combined in activities that lead children to ask questions and discover the why and how of the world for themselves. Stimulating projects are geared to promote creative problem-solving skills, student inventiveness and a good understanding of scientific and technological principles.

Do-it-yourself activities using basic equipment and simple techniques are presented in an easy-to-follow format with at-a-glance informative symbols, extension activities and reproducibles including patent registration forms and evaluation records.

From their baseballs to their bicycles, from their pencils to their computers, children come face to face with contraptions on a daily basis. *Kid Contraptions* gives young inventors the skills they need to explore, understand and become comfortable with existing technology and to recognize the needs and problems of their world. Children will learn to think creatively for challenges of the future as they discover the inventor within!

Sincerely,

Robynne

Robynne Eagan

Symbol Key

These symbols will provide at-a-glance information regarding the preparation of the contraptions.

 Recommended grade level

 Full child participation in preparation

 Partial child participation in preparation

 Caution, adult supervision required

 Ten minutes of active preparation time

Ten to sixty minutes of active preparation time

 Over one hour of active preparation time

Gift

 Large space requirements

 Creative challenge activity

Intensive project
Additional time, materials and assistance may be needed.

 Good group project
Group interaction can be especially valuable in problem-solving activities. Foster idea acceptance and appreciation of one another's input.

 Materials may be difficult to find

Safety

1. Provide students with clear, concise safety rules.
2. Follow instructions carefully.
3. Discuss the sensible use of tools, sharp objects, glass and equipment.
4. Provide ample, flat work space.
5. When necessary, wear a work smock, footwear, safety glasses, earplugs and rubber gloves.
6. Remind students to never put anything in their mouths, eyes or ears.
7. Check the safety of scrap materials. Avoid sharp edges or containers that once held items marked *Keep away from children.* Label all dangerous materials.
8. Always use permanent markers, labeled paints, glues, varnishes and other chemicals in well-ventilated areas.
9. Avoid accidents by maintaining a tidy work area.
10. Use your contraptions wisely. They may break and cause harm if they are pushed beyond their limits.

Aims and Objectives

Activities throughout this resource are designed with the intent to achieve general and specific goals as outlined here.

• •

Aims

To provide the opportunity for children to:

- investigate their environment
- recognize a need for new products
- apply skills and knowledge to solve problems which arise from the needs of peoples and the Earth
- recognize and understand the science of why things happen
- understand how things happen by controlling materials and phenomena
- develop logical thinking and creative problem-solving strategies through a variety of relevant hands-on experiences
- use specific skills to design and make contraptions that will improve the world
- discover concepts and language of science, design and technology
- increase understanding and competence in an ever-changing technological society
- develop confidence in ability to creatively understand, interpret, design and create

• •

Objectives

The child will:

- develop skill in thinking creatively and inventively
- practice various problem-solving strategies
- develop skill in handling various tools, materials and equipment
- be motivated to make discoveries about science and technology
- acquire technological concepts through active learning
- become familiar with the terms and processes of design and technology
- demonstrate an understanding of basic principles of science, design and technology
- develop an understanding of technological development and its impact on society
- use knowledge, skills and creative thinking to respond to a need
- design, plan, make and assess contraptions that really work
- become comfortable with using existing technology

Chapter 1

Let's Get Inventive

What Is a Contraption?

It's a gadget; it's a machine; it's a makeshift kooky device that really works–it's a contraption! Contraptions are in themselves often valuable and useful and many a contraption was the beginning of a great invention.

Humans are always trying to make things better than what exists. Contraptions have made it possible for humans to move heavy loads; send sound and images through wires and across airwaves; build tall structures that reach up, cross over (or under!) large bodies of water, move quickly from one place to another–even outer space!

Many of the things you use every day came from the creative mind of an inventor–like your toothbrush, your pencil, a doorknob, your computer–even your books! There are so many inventions around us that it may seem there is nothing left to invent. Not a chance–humans are always ready for a new gadget, tool, toy, game, computer program, robotic device, vehicle, process, improvement to an existing item or something entirely new. There is always the possibility of something that will make life easier or better–maybe something to help correct problems left by previous inventions!

Great Inventors and the Contraptions That Have Changed Our Lives

Hero, was a famous, first century A.D., Greek engineer and mathematician who wrote books that discussed the lever, pulley, wedge, screw, windlass and the conversion of energy into useful means. He invented a toy called the Aeolipilé that worked by means of jet propulsion–it was the first-known steam turbine.

Archimedes (287 B.C.-212 B.C.) was a brilliant Greek scientist, who invented ideas and machines including the famous Archimedes' Screw.

Leonardo da Vinci (1452-1519) was one of the world's most remarkable inventors. His inventions were so far ahead of their time that the technology to build them was not available. His recorded ideas included flying machines, parachutes, a self-propelling car, a steam engine, a submarine, a paddleboat, a diver's helmet, machine tools and canals.

Isaac Newton (1642-1727): Newton's theories changed the way people looked at the world. He developed rules of calculus and his famous theory of gravity.

Benjamin Franklin (1706-1790): This well-known philosopher, scientist, American statesman and inventor proved that lightning was a discharge of electricity. His many inventions included an improved heating stove and the first lightning rod.

Richard Arkwrithg the Father of the Factory System (1732-1792): Invented the water frame in 1769, a fast-working cotton-spinning machine that could be left to spin by itself. Factories were built for this machine and the Industrial Revolution was underway.

James Watt (1736-1819) invented the first efficient steam engines to meet the need for power during the Industrial Revolution. Factories could work without water, horse or wind power. He coined the word *horsepower* to describe the power of his machine.

Edward Jenner (1749-1823) was an English country physician known as the Father of Immunology. He invented the first vaccine to prevent the deadly smallpox disease in 1796–an invention that effects health and disease control around the world to this day.

Thomas Edison (1847-1931) was one of the world's most successful inventors with over 1,000 patented inventions that changed life in the twentieth century. His inventions include the phonograph (the first record player), the kinetoscope (the first machine film projector), the stock market ticker, improvements to Bell's telephone and his most famous invention–the incandescent carbon filament light bulb.

Alexander Graham Bell (1847-1922) was a teacher of deaf people. His studies of sound led to his invention of the telephone, patented in 1876. This revolutionized long distance communication around the world.

Albert Einstein (1879-1955) was the most well-known inventor of ideas. His creative mathematical and scientific ideas changed the way scientists thought about the universe and gravity. He is well-known for his Special Theory of Relativity and his General Theory of Relativity. His theories inspired one of the major inventions of the twentieth century—nuclear power.

The Wright Brothers flew the first powered plane, near Kitty Hawk, North Carolina, in 1903, and air travel began to take off.

Presper Edkert, Jr. and John Mauchly (University of Pennsylvania engineers) coinvented the first general-purpose electronic digital computer the ENIAC (Electronic Numerical Integrator and Calculator) in1946. It could make 5,000 additions and 300 multiplications per second—the Computer Age was underway.

Marcian Hoff invented the microchip in 1971 at Intel Corporation in Silicon Valley, California. It was to change industry and information technology around the world.

Kids Can Be Inventors, Too!

● ●

Christmas Lights
A terrible fire in 1917 in New York caused by a Christmas tree decorated with candles led 15-year-old Albert Sadacca to invent Christmas tree lights. These didn't sell very well until Albert became the head of a multimillion dollar company.

Toy Truck
In 1963, at the age of six, Buddy Patch got a patent for the toy truck he invented and became one of the youngest inventors ever granted a patent.

Earmuffs
In 1873, in Maine, U.S.A., 15-year-old Chester Greenwood, bent wire into a headband, attached pieces of beaver skin to the sides and invented earmuffs!

Snowmobile
The snowy winters of Quebec led 15-year-old Armand Bombardier to create an unusual motorized sleigh using a car motor and an old airplane propeller and a sleigh. After some improvements to the original design, the snowmobile was patented in 1937.

Calculator
The mathematical genius Blaise Pascal (1623-1662) made the first calculating machine by the time he was 19. A series of gears and wheels and handles added or subtracted up to eight figures. Pascal went on to become a pioneer of hydraulics and pneumatics and set up a public transportation system in Paris using horse-drawn buses.

How to Foster Inventive Thinking

1. Create an emotional atmosphere where children feel secure and free to explore, experiment and try out new ideas. Offer encouragement, praise, consistency and enthusiasm.

2. Provide a stimulating physical learning environment that offers inviting active learning centers and materials.

3. Allow children to help shape the learning environment by being involved in the planning of topics and the physical environment.

4. Provide a wide variety of experiences that will appeal to all kinds of kids. Offer a variety of instructional approaches that allows each child room to learn and create in a manner that best suits them. Provide the materials, then step back and let children investigate and explore.

5. Be prepared before starting an activity. Have materials and set-ups ready so your time can be spent facilitating true learning. Know where the projects are leading before you start and be ready with leading questions, new vocabulary and scientific explorations when opportunities arise.

6. Encourage an investigative approach. Stimulate children to observe, ask questions and use their imaginations, skills and senses to find out for themselves.

7. Lead children to discoveries by offering suggestions or asking leading questions at the appropriate times, such as: What do you think will happen? Why do you suppose. . . ? What did you do? I wonder if. . . ? How can we find out. . . ? etc. Encourage children to think out loud and praise efforts to solve problems.

8. Be open minded and flexible. Follow children's ideas and explanations and allow them to pursue the ideas that are most motivating.

9. Model enthusiasm and creative thinking.

10. Help children to enjoy the discoveries and experience wonder.

Turn Your Classroom into an Invention Lab

Take advantage of children's natural curiosity by providing a stimulating Invention Lab. With the right attitude you can turn *anything* into an invention lab. All you need is an interesting array of materials, a little space to think, create and test inventions and an encouraging atmosphere! Give young inventors a rich array of hands-on activities that allows them to explore, examine, experiment and make new discoveries.

The program and environment should:

- allow for individual creative expression
- provide opportunities to manipulate and explore various materials and tools
- offer developmental lessons with general direction and purpose
- facilitate
- reinforce a child's positive self-concept
- provide experiences which bring satisfaction and joy to the participant

Design and Technology in Education

Design and technology provide relevant, active learning experiences that combine skills, knowledge and problem solving to create a tangible product that solves a perceived human problem or need.

Primary children can be introduced to information technology as a means to record, store or retrieve information. A computer can be used to store or provide information and to reinforce skills and concepts. The telephone or fax can assist in finding resource materials. Calculators can assist with calculations. Familiarization with various equipment will develop competence in the modern world and inspire innovations that will improve existing technology.

Creating Contraptions

ABC

The inventive mind is curious and persistent. Combine knowledge, culture, skills and attitudes about technological development, its use and impact on society into your curriculum. Challenge children to design and produce products that will improve the world in which we live. Children may help to create a better future for us all.

1. **Observe:** Is there a need that you can fulfill? Can you improve upon an existing method? Is there a problem you can solve with an idea, a process or a contraption?

2. **Brainstorm!** Think creatively. How can you solve the problem or meet the need?

3. **Research** and discuss your best solution.

4. **Get Started!** Make, plan and work out the details! How will you make your contraption? What materials will you need? Do you need assistance? Make lists. Think about form, construction, appearance, strength, economy, simplicity, safety and function.

5. **Make It!** Build your contraption; try it out. Learn from mistakes, and remedy any problems.

6. **Evaluate:** Does your contraption solve the problem or meet a need?

7. **Share It!** Demonstrate your contraption. Explain what it does and how it solves a problem or meets a need.

8. Congratulate yourself and move on to a new problem.

Basic Materials, Tools and Equipment

You can create most contraptions with inexpensive household materials, tools and equipment. You will need some basic tools to shape, cut and join various materials. Before you begin, put together a handy Inventors' Kit and a Creators' Corner.

Please exercise caution and common sense when using these materials with small children.

Inventors' Kit

The Inventors' Kit will help children design and build their unique inventions. Put together one large kit or, if your children are old enough, distribute one kit per group within the class. A plastic bin with a lid will work well to contain these items. Each group will assume responsibility for their materials and tools.

Simple Tools

scissors	cool glue gun and	hand drill and drill bits
marking pencil	glue sticks	center punch
paintbrush	metal ruler	adjustable wrench
hammer and nails	sanding block	measuring tape
leather punch	bradawl or knitting needle	small vise that mounts
screwdrivers and screws	junior saw	sturdily to bench
wire cutters	small vise	carpenter's square
craft knife	staplers of various sizes	
file	mitre block	

Basic Materials

marbles or ball bearings	workboard: 15" x 18" (38.1 x 45.72 cm)
wire	of wood, thick cardboard or sturdy
thread	polystyrene
paper fasteners	string
wood dowel	all-purpose and specialized glues
wood pieces of various sizes and	copper wire
shapes	new batteries
masking, electrical, cellophane and	thumbtacks
duct tape	safety glasses
cardboard of various sizes, shapes and	rubber gloves
thickness	hinges
balloons	leather pieces

Enhancement Items

stopwatch	level
computer	paints

Creators' Corner

Collect a wide variety of scrap materials in a series of containers or an area known as the Creators' Corner. See "Materials Worth Scavenging" list for suggestions.

*Add interesting items to the kit and corner as your ideas and needs predict. Find safe substitutes if necessary.

Contraptions Lab Book

Materials:

3-ring binder or duotang
paper
classroom reproducibles (optional)

Process:

1. Educator and children will discuss the concept of contraptions. It will be explained that the Contraptions Lab Book will act as a record of materials, ideas and working models relating to contraptions the child will create.
2. Child will individualize each Contraptions Lab Book with their name and drawing.
3. Child will keep a record of contraptions and related activities within this book in a variety of ways: written record, illustrations, diagrams, photographs, 3-D modeling on paper, reproducibles, etc.
4. Date each page to provide a history of the inventiveness process.

Try This:

- Develop skills in written communication, sketching and early graphing by using the Contraptions Lab Book.
- Make parents aware that this is a working lab book for brainstorming, independent recording and rough drafts. Include a page in the back for parental comments. The book can go between home and school as a form of communication.
- Encourage children to record their inventive ideas before and after the actual model is created. Keep the focus on the actual invention rather than on the record–especially with very young children.

Challenge:

As an inventor, how can you plan, record and save your creations? (Consider paper, recipe cards, chalkboard, 3-D models, oral stories, songs or rhymes, cassettes, videos or computer discs.)

- *Leonardo da Vinci bound his ideas and sketches together in special notebooks. In these books he used elaborate backwards writing that could only be read using a mirror. Why do you think he did this? To keep his ideas secret? For fun? To protect his ideas?*

8

Creative Challenges
Inventive Thinking Motivators

Every activity in this book offers a Creative Challenge geared to inspire the inventive thinking process needed for design and technology. Some activities are simply a Creative Challenge as will be indicated by the symbol 💡. To make the most of these Challenges, provide opportunities for children to explore and express themselves in a way that best suits them: solitary or group investigation, hands on exploration, verbal expression, informative sketches, written record or a working model. Children of any age or ability can respond to challenges at their own level.

Try This:
- Prepare children to be receptive to the ideas of others.
- Model enthusiasm for others' ideas.
- Praise efforts to understand other children's ideas.
- Praise originality and inventive thinking–the more farfetched an idea the better!
- Make children aware that some of the craziest ideas have developed into great inventions.

I Spy

K-3

Materials: Observant children

Process:
1. One child chooses an item within the other children's view. This item must be a part of a working invention in the classroom. This child says, "I spy with my little eye something that is. . . ." Encourage children to look for various pieces that make things work in the classroom, such as the long black arrow (that helps us tell time), the copper hook (that holds our coat) and the white cylinder (that is used to write on the board).
2. This child chooses others to guess the particular item.
3. The child who correctly guesses the chosen item takes over and spies a machine part and the game begins again.

Try This:
- Encourage children to think about the shape, purpose or action of chosen items.

I Can Make It

K-3 · SPACE

An exercise designed to help children gain skill in the basics of observing, planning, interpreting, shaping and joining, and critical analysis.

Materials:

pictures of gadgets and machines (photographs, posters, magazine clippings, etc.)

variety of scrap materials: paper rolls, foam trays, egg cartons, thread spools, pipe cleaners

various tools and creative materials: glue, tape, scissors, rubber bands, joiners, fasteners

flat work surface

Process:

1. Set up centers that offer a variety of interesting scrap materials. At each center display pictures of various inventions, i.e. doorknobs, chimneys, toothbrushes, chairs, binoculars.
2. **Challenge:** Make a model of . . .
3. Children choose a center and look very closely at the object in the picture. What shapes do they spy? What materials will be needed?
4. Children make a model of the object using the scrap materials at their center.
5. Children may put models in a display if they choose.

Try This:

- Encourage students to look carefully at shapes in the picture and shapes of their scrap materials. Ask questions about similar objects that could be made with the particular materials.
- Discuss whether or not the child's model will work like the object in the picture. Why or why not? What might be needed to make the model into a working model?
- Take this opportunity to establish and record children's degree of competency at visualization and with particular tools and materials. What extension activities would be appropriate for their level of development?

10

Keep It Together

Materials:
3' x 2' (.91 m) board of masonite or Plexiglas™
1 container filled with assorted materials: rubber bands, craft sticks, erasers, pencils
string per child or group
small block of paraffin wax

Process:
1. Set the board on a small incline of approximately 40° angle, that allows materials to "slide down the hill."
2. *Challenge:* The materials at the top of this large hill must travel to the bottom of the hill. The materials must stay together for the entire journey.
3. Provide each child or group with the challenge and materials as stated above.
4. Facilitate and allow time for children to discuss and plan, experiment, make mistakes and try again.
5. Have children demonstrate and explain their solutions to the problem.

Try This:
- Students who find a solution before others can be given an additional challenge. Provide them with a stopwatch, and challenge them to find ways to move the materials more quickly.

What Could It Be?

Materials:
containers of various shapes and sizes
record sheet
pencil

Process:
1. Put various containers with the same attributes at several centers.
2. Children proceed to each center with pencil and record sheet.
3. Children explore various containers and record what the container could be.
4. Encourage children to look at the container from various angles. Ask questions such as: Where do we see that shape? What can that shape be used for? Is there anything in your home that has that shape? Where do we see that shape outside?
5. Children record their ideas for later discussion with the group.

Try This:
- Try this activity using gears, hardware, wood scraps, plastic shapes, etc.

Make It Better

1-3

Redesign an everyday household item. You may build a better mousetrap!

Materials: collection of everyday items: cup, pencil, broom, juice jug, telephone
pencil and paper
selection of "junk materials"

Process:

1. As a group, choose one item to make better.
2. Model careful observation and analysis skills. What does this item do? What shape is it? Why is it made this way? Are there any problems with this item?
3. *Challenge:* Make this item better than it is.
4. Encourage students to imagine an ideal item of this nature. What would we like to see it do? Encourage creative, farfetched, innovative ideas. Discuss how this item might be altered to become more like the "ideal" item as imagined by creative thinkers.
5. Assist children as they redesign the item through drawings and exploration of various concrete materials.
6. Provide materials and tools for children to make a "new and improved . . . ."
7. Allow children to present their objects to one another if they choose.

Try This:

- Ask children to bring an ordinary tool, gadget or household contraption. Improve upon these objects. This will help children to look at their own belongings with the eyes of an inventor.
- Take photographs of the improved objects and have children write explanations of their items. Put these photographs and informative paragraphs together in *The New and Improved Book.*

12

Patent Registration Form

Patent Registration Number: _____

Inventor: _____

Name of Contraption: _____

Description: _____

_____

_____

_____

_____

Photo or Sketch

Date: _____

Signature: _____

(Classroom Patent Registration Committee Member)

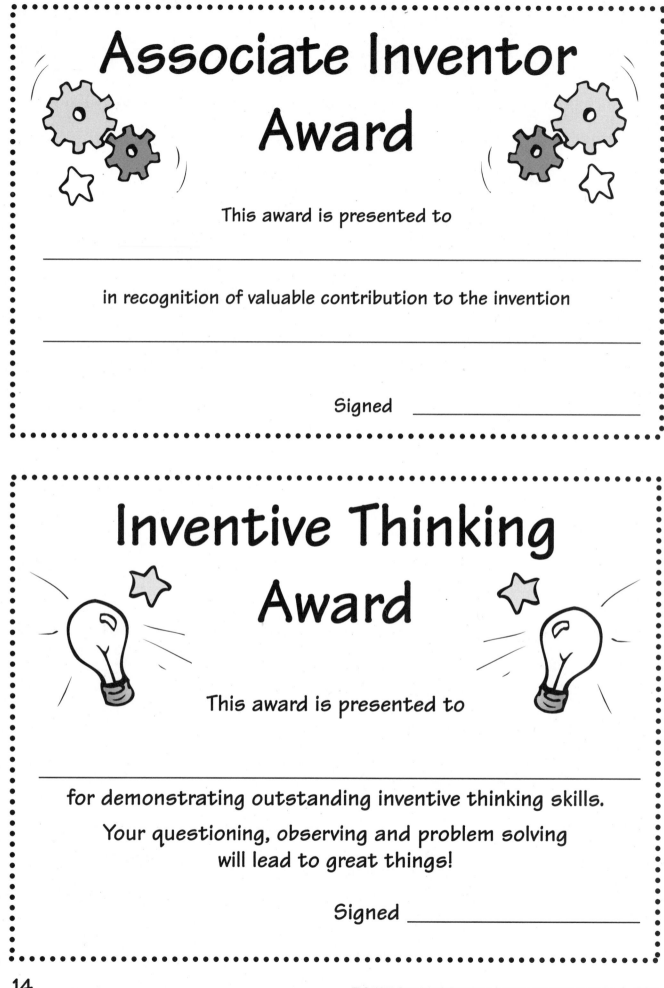

Associate Inventor Award

This award is presented to

_____

in recognition of valuable contribution to the invention

_____

Signed _____

Inventive Thinking Award

This award is presented to

_____

for demonstrating outstanding inventive thinking skills.
Your questioning, observing and problem solving
will lead to great things!

Signed _____

Chapter 2

Machine Mania

. . . .

What Is a Machine?

A machine is the basis for all contraptions. It is a human-made device that makes a task easier. A machine helps us to make better use of force (the push and pull on an object that causes it to move). Some machines are small and simple like a pencil sharpener, that uses a tuning force to cut wood, or a bottle opener or a pair of scissors which use lever action. Some machines are large and complicated like cranes, trains or airplanes. Humans are the only animals to build machines, and we use them to do jobs we can't do by ourselves, like build skyscrapers, lift heavy loads or move us, sometimes faster than the speed of sound, sometimes all the way to outer space!

An automatic or smart machine can work under its own control. To wash your clothes, all you need to do is turn the dial or push a button on the washing machine. A calculator is a small very complex device that helps you to solve math problems quickly with the push of some buttons. Robots are machines that are made to copy human movements. They can do the work of many people or do tasks that people find boring or dangerous.

Simple Machines

All the tools we use around the house are based on six simple machines: lever, pulley, wheel and axle, wedge, screw and inclined plane. Some machines are operated by hand; others are powered by engines or motors. A complex machine or tool consists of two or more simple tools. A pair of scissors is a complex tool consisting of two wedges held together with a screw. The handles act as a lever and force the two wedges through the material being cut.

More power to you! Use a machine to help you cut tin (can opener), lift a car by yourself (car jack), pull a nail from a piece of wood (curved lever, claw hammer), split apart wire (wire snips), tighten metal on metal (wrench), remove lids (screw), break apart wood (wedge, axe), move yourself and heavy things to high places (stairs and ramps) and move yourself quickly (wheel and axle).

Machines Are Everywhere!

Find and circle the machines in this picture.

lever   inclined plane   pulley

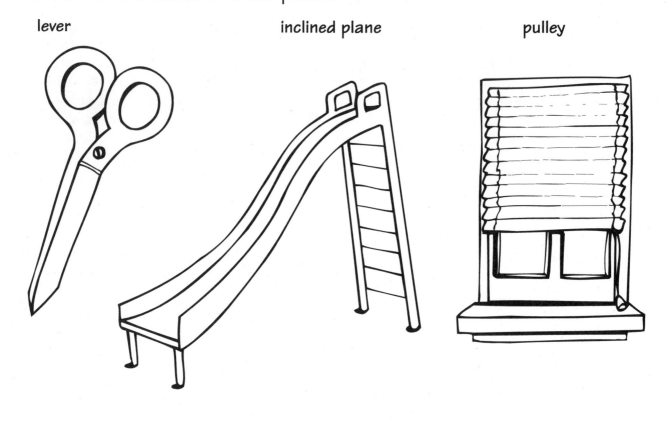

wedge   wheel and axle   screw

Machine Hunt

💡 K-3 🍪

A great way to open children's eyes to the machines around them.

Materials: school, home or neighborhood
investigative, observant children

Process:

1. Introduce the concept of a machine as something that makes a task easier.
2. *Challenge:* Find as many machines as you can.
3. Take a walk around a home, school or neighborhood. Encourage children to look at small and large, simple or complex items.
4. Return to the class to list and discuss the many machines. This is a wonderful opportunity to make children aware of the attributes and various types of machines. Ask questions such as: How is that machine like the one Billy saw? How does that machine make life easier or better?

Try This:

- Can children identify what simple machine or machines are incorporated into the device? Think about the parts that do the work and draw that part.
- Photograph or sketch the various machines for a bulletin board display.
- Provide a Take Apart Center where children can take the covers off machines and look inside to see the way a machine works. Try a clock, pencil sharpener, electric car, etc.
- Research or make up a story about the inventor of a particular machine. What need was perceived? How did the idea originate? What was the first model made of?

Marble Maze

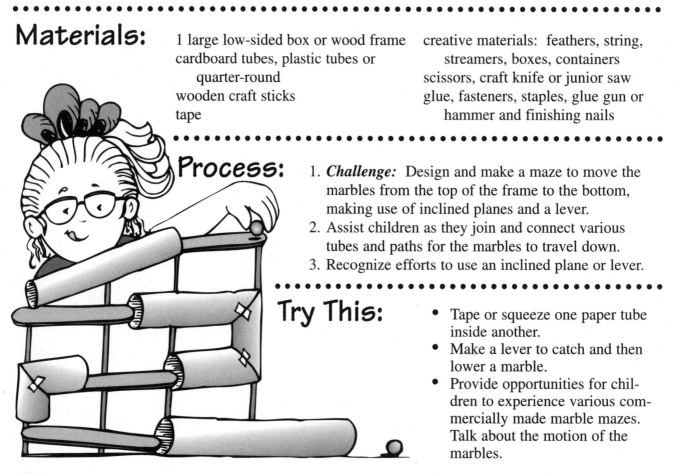

A contraption that uses all kinds of materials and all types of machines.

A **lever** is a simple machine used to make work easier by helping us to lift or move heavy loads with little effort or to act as a prying device. It consists of a lifting piece and a stationary or pivot point known as the fulcrum (i.e. the screw on scissors or the point where the hammer head rests on a board). Force on one end of a lever causes the other end to go up with greater force to lift a load, turn a bolt or pry into something. A clawed hammer and crowbar are simple levers, pliers or a pair of scissors are double levers.

An **inclined plane** is a simple machine that can be used to raise an object from one level to another with less force. It is a slanting surface that helps to move things up or down. Stairs, sloping floors and ramps are inclined planes.

A **screw** is a special kind of inclined plane that spirals around a center rod. It is used for raising things like the lid on a jar, piano stool or auger. It also holds things together in its common form as a wood or metal screw.

A **wedge** has a slanted inclined plane that ends in a sharp thin end. It is used for cutting and prying things apart. Knives and axes, scissors and needles are wedges.

Materials:

1 large low-sided box or wood frame
cardboard tubes, plastic tubes or
    quarter-round
wooden craft sticks
tape

creative materials: feathers, string,
    streamers, boxes, containers
scissors, craft knife or junior saw
glue, fasteners, staples, glue gun or
    hammer and finishing nails

Process:

1. *Challenge:* Design and make a maze to move the marbles from the top of the frame to the bottom, making use of inclined planes and a lever.
2. Assist children as they join and connect various tubes and paths for the marbles to travel down.
3. Recognize efforts to use an inclined plane or lever.

Try This:

- Tape or squeeze one paper tube inside another.
- Make a lever to catch and then lower a marble.
- Provide opportunities for children to experience various commercially made marble mazes. Talk about the motion of the marbles.

Shoe Racers

K-3   Caution

Recycled, inventive contraptions for hours of fun.

. . . .

A **wheel and axle** is a simple machine used to move things. The wheel is a circle with a hub or center where a rod or axle goes through. The wheel rotates around the axle as you see with a rolling pin.

. . . .

Materials:

old shoe   thread spools
coat hanger or similar wire   packing tape
bead spacers

. . . .

Process:

1. *Challenge:* Using these materials, make a vehicle that can be raced.
2. Provide the materials and the Challenge and allow children to discover problems and solutions for themselves as they design and build their vehicles.
3. Encourage children to examine the materials and plan a vehicle before beginning. Drawings may be helpful.
4. Ask leading questions: Will the wheels turn? Does the vehicle need something to hold the wheels? How can we attach the axle? How will the wheels stay on the vehicle? How many wheels does the vehicle need? How can we test our ideas?
5. Introduce new vocabulary–wheels, axle, wire snips, spacer, rotate. . . .

. . . .

Try This:

• Incorporate an art lesson. Make the racers sporty with decorations of all kinds–paints, stickers, ribbons, balloon bumpers, flags, fabric paints, neon headlights, etc. Be creative!
• Make a "driver" for the racer. Plush characters, plastic figures or paper personalities will bring the race to life. The cut off end of a balloon makes a nifty racing helmet.
• Make an inclined plane racetrack for the racers. Separate tracks with a shoelace lane marker hot glued to the track. Decorate the track with flags, toothpick and gumdrop stands and structures.
• Host a Big Race Day and set up a Sporty Racers display.
• Make a simple wheel by cutting out a cardboard circle and pushing a pencil through the center. Friction prevents it from spinning quickly.

* Caution: Be careful with wire snips and glue gun.

. . . .

Challenge:

For advanced children: Make your vehicle go faster. Can you measure the speed of the vehicle? Provide a stopwatch and a means to measure and mark the track.

Gear Up

1-3

Gears are wheels with teeth used to transfer force from one part of a machine to another. The teeth mesh, or fit together so one wheel can turn another wheel to make a task easier. Sometimes one wheel turns another with a belt or a drive chain like on a bicycle.

Materials:

heavy cardboard
 (at least ³/₈" [.95 cm])
craft knife
cutting mat
mounting board of cardboard
thumbtacks of finishing nails
compass to draw circles

Process:

1. Design and pencil in gears.
2. Cut these on a cutting mat.
3. Mount the gears on a heavy sheet of cardboard so that each gear turns the next.

Try This:

- Introduce a tiny drive chain (of paper clips) to fit around the teeth, now called sprockets.
- Investigate the drive chain on a bicycle.
- Research the fascinating invention of the bicycle from the first pedalless wooden dandy horse in 1817 to the modern racing cycles of today.
- Investigate a hand-held eggbeater. Crank the handle and watch the motion transfer to two wheels that whirl in opposite directions to make a job easier.
- Look at the crank-operated pencil sharpener.

* Caution: Be careful when cutting.

Challenge:

Make one gear with ten teeth and one gear, half the radius of the larger, with five teeth. The teeth should be the same size on both gears. If the large gear makes seven revolutions, how many revolutions does the small gear make?

Thread Spool, Box and String Crane

2-3

A **pulley** is a simple machine that helps lift things by increasing and changing the direction of force. It is a special grooved wheel turned by a rope or drive belt. A series of pulleys provides a mechanical advantage that allows work to be done with less effort.

Materials:

2' (.61 m) string
4" (10.16 cm) string
hammer and two nails that are longer
    than the length of the spools
tape
paper clip
2 thread spools
scissors, junior saw or craft knife
plastic tub or other small container
piece of wood
cargo
strong cardboard box
    (about the size of a shoe box)
handle: dowel and wood strip
2' x 2' piece of balsa wood
    (about 24" [.61 m] long)

Process:

1. Mark and cut a hole in the box to snugly position the wooden "boom" so that one end is supported against the inside of the box and the other end protrudes at approximately a 45° angle, about 6" (15.24 cm) beyond the base box.
2. Temporarily position the "boom" and pencil mark about 1¹/₂" from the base box up the "boom" and ¹/₄" from the end of the "boom" on the same side.
3. Remove the "boom" and nail one spool at each marked position. Ensure that the spool turns freely. Replace the "boom" in the hole.
4. Using the 4" (10.16 cm) string and tape, make a handle like that on a pail for the lifting container. Try lifting it. Reposition the handle if necessary.
5. Poke a pencil or small wood strip into the lower spool to form a crank.
6. Tape one end of the 2' (.61 m) string to the lower spool. Wind the string around the spool.
7. Bring the other end of the string over the top spool and attach a paper clip hook.
8. Wind the other end of the string onto the lower spool.
9. Fill lifting container with the cargo and hook the container to the crane.
10. Wind the handle and watch the cargo rise.

Try This:

- Discuss how a pulley can help to lift a heavy load as the upper spool transfers the downward force of the children's actions on the handle into the upward lift that raises the load.
- Add a weight to the top of the box or L-support if the need for counter-weight arises.
- Put a magnet in place of the hook and watch the crane pick up the magnetic items.

*   Caution: Be careful using tools.

• •

Challenge:

Make a pulley. Provide wire, thread spools, string, hooks and heavy objects.

• •

My Machine

1-3

Invent a new machine of your own!

• •

Materials:

paper and pencil

• •

Process:

1. Discuss machines and inventions. Is there a need for something? A need to do something better, easier or faster?
2. *Challenge:* Design a new machine.
3. Name the machine and sketch and describe it in your Contraptions Lab Book. Explain what the machine does and what makes it work.

• •

Try This:

- Present machines to one another.
- Make your machine with your Inventors' Kit and scrap materials. Take photographs.
- File a Patent Registration Form in your classroom.
- Make a bulletin board display of the machine designs. Add gears and pulleys around the border to make the display more interesting.
- Most machines help to make our lives better at the particular point in time. Discuss the ways that some machines have made the quality of our lives worse. Consider pollution and weapons.

Chapter 3

Energy Transfer and Complex Mechanical Machines

Make the most of your contraptions with energy transfer, the basis for movement in machines!

Potential energy, as is stored in our muscles or in fuels, allows us to apply force to move things. Potential energy can be transferred from these sources to make contraptions move in particular ways.

Many machines are powered by motors, complicated contraptions that change potential energy into movement (kinetic energy). Various mechanisms allow machines to turn one kind of motion into another and apply just the right amount of force in just the right place.

Energy Transfer

K-3

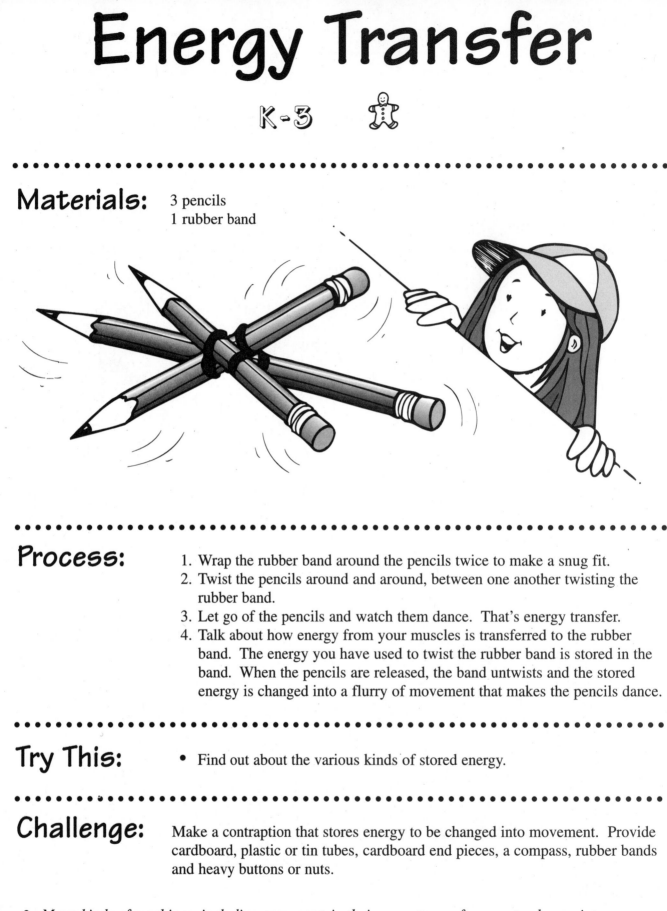

Materials: 3 pencils
1 rubber band

Process:
1. Wrap the rubber band around the pencils twice to make a snug fit.
2. Twist the pencils around and around, between one another twisting the rubber band.
3. Let go of the pencils and watch them dance. That's energy transfer.
4. Talk about how energy from your muscles is transferred to the rubber band. The energy you have used to twist the rubber band is stored in the band. When the pencils are released, the band untwists and the stored energy is changed into a flurry of movement that makes the pencils dance.

Try This:
• Find out about the various kinds of stored energy.

Challenge: Make a contraption that stores energy to be changed into movement. Provide cardboard, plastic or tin tubes, cardboard end pieces, a compass, rubber bands and heavy buttons or nuts.

• *Many kinds of machines, including cars, contain their own stores of energy to change into movement. The energy for a car is supplied in the form of fuel that is changed into forward or backward movement.*

Friction Fighters

K-3   10 min

....

Friction: Whenever anything moves on Earth, it encounters a force of resistance called friction. Friction opposes motion and causes moving objects to slow down and eventually stop. It produces heat and wear and hinders the operation of machines. Inventors look for ways to reduce friction between the moving parts of a machine. Oil and ball bearings are used in various contraptions to reduce friction.

When you go down a slide, the force of gravity gets you going. Gravity also makes you accelerate as you go down the slide while the force of friction makes you slow down and eventually stop.

....

Materials:

book	6 pencils	3 jar lids of different
rubber bands	15 marbles the same	sizes
paper clips	size	table

....

Process:

1. Put a rubber band around the book. Hook the paper clip to the band on one end of the book.
2. Move the book across the table using the hook. Ask "How did you move the book?" Encourage children to talk about pushing or pulling the book–applying force.
3. Ask "Did the book move easily? What is preventing the book from moving freely?"
4. *Challenge:* Move the book using the lid, pencils and marbles.
5. Encourage all methods of movement. Ask "How does this motion feel compared to before? What else can you try? Why do you think that works?" Lead children to understand that rolling items reduces friction.

....

Try This:

- Investigate friction. Move things on rough and smooth surfaces.
- Rub two blocks of wood together. How do they feel? Friction produces heat.
- Friction produces wear. Look for signs of friction (shoes, erasers, paths, flooring).
- Wheels that move fast have ball bearings around their axles. Investigate the wheels of bicycles, automobiles, electric fans, food mixers and roller skates. Display commercial ball bearings. Discuss how ball bearings roll against an axle and cut down on friction. Listen for ball bearings in the wheels of a roller skate or skateboard.
- Provide 15 marbles the same size and three jar lids of different sizes. Put the smallest lid inside the middle-sized lid. Put a ring of marbles around the edge of the small lid and put the large lid over the top. Put a book on the lid and spin it.
- The first wheel was probably a rolling log. How could that have come about?

Safe Landing Contraption

A contraption that tames the force of gravity with air friction.

Materials:

large square of cloth or plastic
4 lengths of string about 20"
    (50.8 cm) long
small light weight: cloth doll,
    plastic figurine or washer

Process:

1. Tie one string to each corner of your cloth.
2. Tie the four ends of string into a knot.
3. Attach a parachutist to the knot.
4. Hang the cloth from its center point.
5. With a swinging motion, toss the parachute into the air and watch it float back down.
6. Discuss the way gravity pulls the parachutist to the ground while air friction on the parachute opposes gravity making for a safe landing.

Try This:

• Parachutes can control their descent by using cords to vary the air flow in the parachute.
• Talk about another contraption that uses friction–brakes! The harder the brake presses on the wheel, the slower the vehicle goes. Test it out on bicycles.

Challenge:

Design another contraption that *uses* friction.

Old-Fashioned Waterwheel

Materials:

water hose or tube attached
    to a tap
water center or outdoor space
PVC pipe (6"-12"
    [15.24-30.48 cm] long)
2 ice cream container lids
polystyrene trays
water-resistant glue (cool
    glue gun and glue sticks)
string or dowelling to fit
    inside the PVC pipe
set of compasses

Process:

1. Mark and drill a center hole to fit the PVC pipe on the two container lids.
2. Cut four 2" (5.08 cm) slats of polystyrene to fit from the center of the lid to the outside edge.
3. Mark the center of the PVC pipe.
4. Put one lid onto the PVC. Glue it 1" (2.54 cm) from the center line.
5. Glue the four slats, equal distances apart, to the lid and the PVC pipe.
6. Glue the second lid on top of the slats and to the PVC pipe.
7. When the glue has thoroughly bonded, put the dowelling through the center of the pipe and move the contraption to a water table, sink or outdoor space.
8. Place the dowelling ends on top of two pails or large tin cans and secure with tape or hold in a stable position.
9. Position a water source directly above the waterwheel.
10. Watch the wheel go around.

Try This:

• Move water. Place a small pail where it can be filled by the wheel, and watch the water move from the hose to the pail.

* Caution: Be careful when cutting wood pieces.

Challenge:

Design a boat that is powered by the "waterwheel."

Cork Rocket

K-3

Pneumatics at work!

Materials:

wet tissue paper
plastic bottle with small opening

Process:

1. Wet the tissue paper and shape it into a cork rocket.
2. Plug the top of the bottle with the cork rocket.
3. Squeeze the bottle hard.
4. Observe and discuss what happened. Why did the cork fly out? What happened to the air inside the bottle? What happened when the air was compressed too much?

Try This:

- Measure how far the cork flies.
- Discuss why the cork didn't continue to rocket through the air. What force slowed the rocket down? What would happen if you sent this rocket sailing off into space where there is no gravity?
- Pour 1/8 cup (30 ml) of baking soda into the bottle. Add 1/2 cup (120 ml) vinegar. Cork it quickly and watch the rocket!

Challenge:

How can you make the cork go faster? Can you invent a method to measure how fast the cork is travelling? Provide a stopwatch and measuring device.

Harness the Wind!

· ·

1. Cut on the dotted lines
2. Fold A, B, C and D into the center dot.
3. Put a fastener or a pin through the center.
4. Attach the wheel to a plastic balloon stick, pencil or wooden dowel using a pin or fastener.
5. Blow on it or hold it into the wind and watch it go!

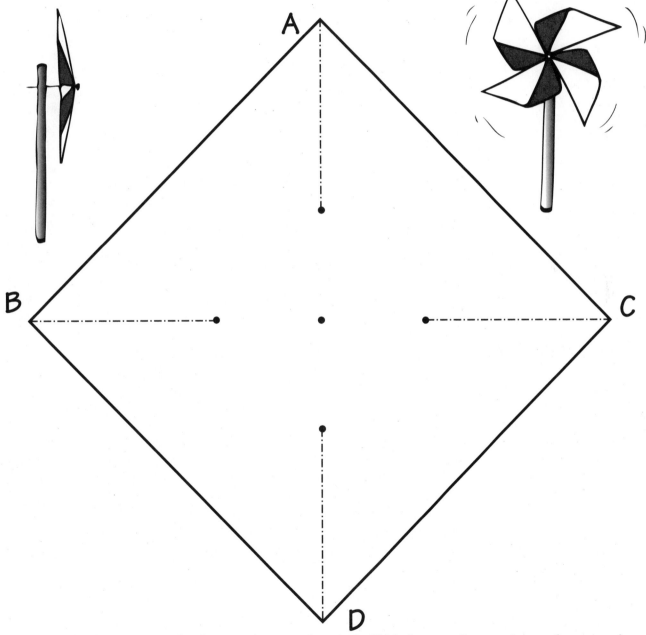

- *Leonardo da Vinci was the first person to make windmill blades turn from an internal source of power. He speculated that a windmill in reverse could be useful. From the windmill, Da Vinci invented the helicopter in the 1400s. Five hundred years later, in 1919, a working helicopter was finally built.*

Hovercraft

A wind-powered wonder.

Materials:

sturdy cardboard
darning needle
compass
balloon

plastic tubing wide enough for neck
of a balloon to fit tightly over
cool glue gun and glue sticks

Process:

1. Cut a circle out of the cardboard about 4" (10.16 cm) across. Do not let the cardboard get crumpled or bent.
2. Make a small hole in the center with the needle.
3. Glue a 2" (5.08 cm) section of tubing above the hole in the card and let it dry.
4. Inflate the balloon and fit the neck over the free end of the tube.
5. Place the contraption on a smooth, flat surface and watch it float on a cushion of air.
6. Discuss how the air that is expelled from the balloon spreads out beneath the contraption and raises it above the surface. The air cushion between the table and the flat surface of the card experience very little friction and allows the contraption to move easily.

Try This:

- Learn about the hovercraft. Christopher Cockerell invented a model of the hovercraft using tin cans. It worked and in 1955 the tin can model became the hovercraft which focuses air beneath its hull so it can float over the land, snow, ice or water.
- Write a story about where you would go if you had a hovercraft.
- Discuss the merits of the hovercraft. Why do you think its use is limited?

* Caution: Be careful when using the needle, compass and glue gun.

Challenge:

Design a contraption that uses this technology.

Water Spinner

1-3   🐛   ⏱10-60 min.   ⚠Caution

A real motor!

Materials:

tin can with base
nail
hammer
block
2 bendy straws cut to
    about 3" (7.62 cm)
plasticene or bubble gum
sturdy, lightweight string
pouring container
water

Process:

1. Using the hammer, nail and block (held inside), make two small holes on opposite sides of the can about 1/2" (1.25 cm) from the top.
2. Thread and knot string through the holes so the can will be suspended in the air.
3. Make two holes on either side of the can about 1/2" (1.25 cm) from the base.
4. Push the straws into the holes so that the bended end protrudes from the can. Bend the ends so that both are pointing clockwise.
5. Seal the joints with plasticine or chewed bubble gum.
6. Suspend the can from the strings and place it over a water table or take it outdoors.
7. Pour water into the can and watch it spin around as water empties through the straws.
8. Discuss the pushing force caused by the water pouring from the straws.

Try This:

• Some machines are supplied with electric energy, others with fuel. What powers this contraption? Help children understand that the energy comes from flowing water.
• Provide the opportunity for students to explore at a water table with a waterwheel, hand pump, pouring containers and droppers.

* Caution: Be careful when making holes.

Challenge:

Make a contraption powered by flowing water. Provide waterproof containers and materials, a water table or outdoor environment, pouring containers and a flowing tap or hose.

• *Hydroelectricity is a form of electricity produced by the energy of flowing water.*

Electric Energy

The simple circuit that really works!

Materials:

2 pieces plastic-coated wire at least
　6" (15.24 cm) long
1.5-3.0 volt flashlight bulb
bulb holder
1.5 volt battery (AA, C or D cell)

small screwdriver
mounting board
Mac-tak™ or plasticine
tape, pipe cleaner or rubber band for
　mounting battery

Process:

1. Discuss places where electricity is used in our lives.
2. Put the bulb in the bulb holder.
3. Strip the wire so that the inner strands of metal are showing at both ends.
4. Attach two wire ends to the screws on the bulb holder.
5. Attach loose ends of other wires to battery and light things up.

Try This:

- What else could be used in place of the light bulb? A buzzer?
- Use the switch to send coded messages to friends.
- Look at the wire and the bulb with a magnifying glass. What do you see inside the bulb.
- Look around! Make a list of all the things that work because of electricity.
- Discuss safety issues regarding electricity. Make some posters.
- Research some of Benjamin Franklin's inventions. He was one of the first people to experiment with electricity.

* Caution: Battery power is weak compared to the electricity we use on a daily basis. Make children aware that electricity in our homes is much more powerful and extremely dangerous. Remind them to never play with electric outlets or appliances.
* Caution: Never use old batteries. Warn children to beware of split or leaking batteries.

Challenge:

Make an On/Off switch by wrapping the wire around a paper clip. Touching the paper clip to the battery will light the bulb. Devise a switch method to turn the light on and off by moving the paper clip.

- *Electricity used to light a bulb moves through the wires and bulbs all around the circuit–it is called electric current.*
- *A battery is a special device that contains electricity-producing chemicals. Alessandro Volta invented the first electric battery (the voltaic pile) in 1800.*

Chapter 4

Contraptions for Comfort

Contraptions for Comfort

Human beings are always trying to make things a little better than they are. Many contraptions are invented to meet our basic needs for shelter, food and water, warmth and comfort.

Let's Make a Shelter

Materials:

large cardboard boxes
sheets of cardboard
cardboard tubes

cloth sheets
wide masking tape
scissors

Process:

1. Discuss animal and human shelters. What is their main purpose? What elements are necessary?
2. **Challenge:** Build a shelter that you can fit in.
3. Provide construction materials and stand back. This should be an open-ended project where children discover questions and problem solve.
4. Ask leading questions such as: "Who needs a shelter? Why? What parts might a shelter need? Why might we need something above our heads? How can we join pieces together? Can we get in and out of this shelter?"
5. Visit and enjoy one another's structures.

Try This:

- Before building their structure, have children use toy building blocks or skewers and gumdrops to build shelters for toy animals and people.
- Take another look at these houses. What could be added? Is there a window, door, curtain, paint or siding, furniture, garden, decorations, etc.? Add these.
- Take a look at interior design. Discuss home, school, color, shape, light and texture.

* Caution: Be careful using scissors on heavy cardboard.

- *A structure provides support and must be able to resist forces; it must support its own weight as well as other weights it is designed to support.*

Caught in the Rain

K-3 ☺ 10-60 min. ⚠ Caution

Materials:

school backpack
papers
tape

book
plastic garbage bag

Process:

1. Provide each group with a school backpack to investigate.
2. Set up a role-playing situation in which children are walking home from school and get caught in a rainstorm.
3. **Challenge:** Use the items in your backpack to help keep you dry.
4. Allow children to use the backpack and items within it any way possible to keep themselves dry.
5. After the "rain," share ideas about how items were used.

Try This:

- Supply materials to make a new improved umbrella.
- Test various materials in a water table. What materials would keep you dry in a rainstorm?
- Sit in a circle and make rain. Each child copies what the person to their right is doing. The leader goes through a series of actions: blow gently (wind), tap fingers together (the first raindrops), clap hands (the rain).

* Caution: Be careful with plastic bag.

- *In the thirteenth century, South American Indians used rubber sap to waterproof clothing.*
- *The first raincoat was invented by Scottish chemist, Charles Macintosh in 1823. A layer of rubber between two pieces of wool cloth became a waterproof fabric that was made into the famous macintosh raincoat.*

Shoe-for-All

K-3 ☆ Caution

Materials:

collection of interesting shoes and boots
assorted interesting materials and fabrics
scissors
cool glue gun and glue sticks
adhesive tape

Process:

1. Set up shoe centers with a variety of shoes and materials at each.
2. **Challenge:** Interesting characters are in need of footwear. Design and make a shoe just for them. Consider a ballerina on a muddy stage, an alien on a planet covered with rubber, an astronaut who keeps floating off the moon or a child who must jump over small streams to get to school.
3. Allow children the opportunity to create footwear for the various characters.
4. Children present their shoe and its attributes.
5. Children take a critical look at each other's shoes and discuss.

Try This:

• Create a Shoe-for-All display. Label each shoe.
• Allow children to invent their own unusual characters in need of footwear.
• Children can create the perfect shoe for a parent or friend for Mother's Day, Father's Day or a birthday. The shoe will be a reflection of the individual's personality, interests and needs.
• Encourage children to experiment with various materials, tools and equipment as they create.
• Incorporate this activity with language arts and design shoes for characters in a book.

* Caution: Be careful when using the glue gun.

• *A 20-year-old cloth seller in New York was attracted by the Gold Rush of 1848. He took a few bolts of cloth to sell on the journey west. He sold everything but a roll of canvas. No one wanted clothes made out of canvas, but it turned out that "up in the diggin's" where the miners worked, pants wore out very quickly. Levi Strauss made some pairs of canvas trousers to sell to miners. It wasn't long before he forgot all about gold digging–he called his pants Levi's, and they were popular with miners and cowboys. Today they are popular with everyone around the globe.*

Creative Hinges

 1-3 🍪 ⏱

Materials:

small cardboard box	string	pipe cleaners
scissors	paper fasteners	leather
adhesive tape	single-hole punch	eye screws

Process:

1. Look at hinges around the school.
2. Discuss the different types of hinges.
3. *Challenge:* Design your own unique hinge for a door or window on the structure.
4. Provide the materials and facilitate learning where possible.
5. Observe one another's hinges and discuss the merits and problems of each.

Try This:

- Start a hinge collection in your classroom.
- Have a Hinge Hunt throughout the school. How many hinges can you find?

- *The earliest-known metal hinges were found in Tutankhamun's tomb dating from 1350 B.C.*

Hand Warmers

 K-3 🍪 ⏱

Materials:

felt, cotton, fur, fleece	glue
pieces of fluffy imitation fur	needle and thread
wire	warm potatoes or boiled eggs
scissors	plastic containers holding warm water

Process:

1. *Challenge:* Invent a new way to keep hands warm
2. Provide the materials and the Challenge and facilitate inventive thinking!

Try This:

- Encourage children to use their Contraptions Lab Book to plan and design their new hand warmers.
- Ask about the practicality, appearance, costs of the hand warmer.
- Integrate this activity with a winter unit.

* Caution: Be careful when using the needle.

"Fan"tastic

1-3

Just the contraption for a hot day!

Materials:

8½" x 11" (21.6 x 27.94 cm) paper per child
single-hole punch
yarn
crayons

Process:

1. Decorate paper with colorful patterns.
2. Begin with the 8" (20.32 cm) side of the paper, and fold a strip approximately 1" (2.54 cm) wide.
3. Flip the paper over and fold it back another 1" (2.54 cm)–accordion style.
4. Continue flipping the paper and folding until all of the paper is folded into creases.
5. Tape the bottom outside flaps and allow the top to expand.
6. Punch a hole in the bottom edge.
7. Thread a string through the hole and tie.
8. Use the fan to cool yourself down on a hot day.
9. Wear the fan around your wrist when not in use.

Try This:

- Make fans of various shapes and sizes.
- Ask "Where does the power come from to make this fan work?"
- Research and discuss the effects of the various cooling techniques on the environment. Make children aware of all of these factors, and then design a graph to show which cooling method children prefer.

Challenge:

Using the Creators' Corner and the Inventors' Kit, design a new method to cool people down on a hot day.

- *When Schuyler S. Wheeler invented the electric fan to cool people down, it was a most welcome advancement over the hand-held fan. What invention is replacing the electric fan today?*

Toothbrushing Timer

 K-3

Materials: 2 clear plastic bottles
duct tape

rice, popcorn kernels or mini pasta
stopwatch

Process:

1. Fill one bottle about half full of rice, popcorn kernels or mini pasta.
2. Hold the second bottle upside down, joining the necks of the bottles together.
3. Use duct tape to make a secure seal between the two bottles.
4. Turn the timer over and using the stopwatch measure how long it takes for the contents to empty into the lower bottle.
5. *Challenge:* Adjust the bottles and contents to take about two minutes to empty–the time recommended for proper brushing of the upper or lower set of teeth. (Flip the timer and brush the other row for the same amount of time.)
6. *Challenge:* Find a use for your timer. Incorporate it into another invention.

Try This:

- Make a toothbrush holder to go with your toothbrushing timer. Discuss the problems of a wet environment and germs and the need to separate brushes from one another.
- Integrate with a health theme.

Kid Chair

💡 2-3 🍪 ⚠️ Caution

Materials:

samples or magazine photographs of
   many types of chairs
Inventors' Kit

Creators' Corner
skewers, toothpicks and gumdrops
PVC pipe and joints

Process:

1. *Challenge:* Most furniture is made to be comfortable for adults. Design a model of a chair that would be just right for kids.
2. Provide the materials and the Challenge.
3. Provide the opportunity for children to sample various kinds of chairs: children's school chair, molded and wooden chairs, swivel chair, recliner, orthopedic chair, stool, hair salon chair, beanbag chair and swinging basket chair. Provide magazine photos if the real experience isn't possible.
4. Encourage children to plan their design in their Contraptions Lab Book.
5. Provide materials and adult assistance where necessary for children to construct models of their perfect Kid Chair.

Try This:

- Ask a physiotherapist or chiropractor to visit your class to talk about chairs, body positions and potential aches and pains.
- Visit a furniture store to look at chairs.
- Design a water chair. What problems must be overcome? Make a small prototype using water-filled balloons or rubber gloves.

* Caution: Be careful when using tools and equipment.

Lights Out

💡 2-3 🍪 ⚠️ Caution

Materials:

10' (3 m) of string
tape

light switch
door with a doorknob

chair, desk or bed leg

Process:

1. *Challenge:* You are an avid bookworm and want to read into the night. Design and construct a system that will turn the lights out when Mom or Dad opens the door to check on you.
2. Provide the Challenge and materials, and let children investigate possible solutions.

Try This:

- Present this as a take-home project. Students can learn to map and sketch an accurate representation of their bedrooms and the mechanism of their Lights Out contraption.
- Are there other solutions to this problem that require a different set of materials?

* Caution: String should never be attached where it could present a risk of strangulation.

Earth Care

Our comfort depends on it! Challenge children to be aware of and to solve some pressing environmental problems. Design and technology should be used to care for and use our environment in a responsible manner as the needs and problems of human beings are being addressed.

Edible Dishes

💡   K-3   🍪   ⏱   🛒

Help save the Earth with garbage-free food.

Materials:
lettuce or cabbage leaves
crepes
waffles
pastry dough
rolling pin
scooped out fruit or vegetables (tomatoes, mushrooms, melons, etc.)
royal icing: 2 egg whites, ½ tsp. (2.5 ml) cream of tartar, 3 cups (720 ml) sifted icing sugar, 1 tsp. (5 ml) vanilla. Beat egg whites until frothy; add cream of tartar; beat again; gradually add icing sugar. Keep covered with a damp cloth. Makes a great cement!

Process:
1. Discuss the problems with the garbage produced by most convenience foods.
2. Brainstorm for examples of foods that do not come with excess packaging. Look for an opportunity to introduce the concept of edible dishes.
3. *Challenge:* Invent an edible food container.
4. Provide the materials above and the Challenge.
5. Allow children to explore with the materials and design and construct an edible food container.
6. Share these inventions with one another. Encourage discussion.

Try This:
- Set up a display of the edible dishes.
- Set up a trial of the various dishes, maybe at lunch or snack time. Ask children to evaluate the various dishes.
- *Challenge:* Design and make a model of a contraption that will produce your edible food containers.

- *Ice-Cream Cone: Charles Menches sold ice cream in dishes until a hot August day at the height of the Louisiana Purchase Exposition when he ran out of dishes. Ernest Hamwi was selling Middle Eastern Zalabia, a crisp wafer-like pastry sold with syrup. Menches rolled up Zalabia, scooped his ice cream on top and ice-cream cones were born!*

Recycling Center

Materials: Inventors' Kit and Creators' Corner   plastic or wood pieces for dividers
large containers

Process:

1. Discuss problems with recycling in the home, school, workplace, mall or local restaurant.
2. Brainstorm for solutions to some of the problems with storage and cleanliness of the various recycled materials. Discuss the need to separate particular materials, the space requirements of some materials, the problems with removing staples and the cleaning of containers.
3. *Challenge:* Design and construct a working model of a recycling center that could be used in any home.
4. Provide materials and assistance to enable children to construct a solution to a real-life problem.

Try This:

- Look at various existing methods of storage of recyclables.
- Collect food packaging from all students for one week–the mountain of excess packaging will be an eye-opener that illustrates a need in our society.

* Caution: Be careful when using tools.

Compost Creature

 2-3 🛒

Reduce your garbage and feed your garden!

Materials:
rotting organic materials
soil
various wood, plastic or wire containers, large drums, barrels or snow fencing

Process:

1. Discuss the benefits of saving organic material.
2. Talk about the problems of saving organic material.
3. Brainstorm together to find some possible solutions to this real-life problem.
4. *Challenge:* Invent a Compost Creature that turns food scraps into rich organic fertilizer.
5. Encourage students to think about appearance, space requirements and potential odors or rodent attraction.
6. Test the various models in your school throughout the year. Fill the container with grass cuttings, food scraps, wood ashes, dead leaves or any other organic material you can find. (Avoid meat, dairy products and the insides of the egg.) Watch the materials disintegrate into fine, soil particles rich in the elements needed for plant growth.

Try This:

- Invite a gardener to your class to discuss various methods of composting and the benefits to the lawn, garden and produce.
- Invite a waste management representative from your neighborhood to discuss the benefits of reducing the amount of garbage you send to the curb.
- Begin this project on Earth Day.
- Invite adults to assist in the making of various composters.
- Raise funds for school activities or to donate to an environmental cause by selling this valuable composted material or by constructing and selling the composters.

Chapter 5

Communication Contraptions

Let's Communicate!

Communication is the exchange of thoughts, feelings and ideas. Humans communicate through symbols, gestures, signals, signs, the printed word, sounds and spoken words. Down through the ages a multitude of contraptions have helped us communicate better. Today we can communicate large quantities of information through various media, we can send messages all over the world very quickly, and we can talk to and see people even if they are on the other side of the world!

Communication with Sound Contraptions

We hear sounds with our ears and special equipment that can help us hear very soft sounds. People all over the world communicate many things with various kinds of sound.

Get the Message

Put a circle around each place where communication is happening in this picture.

Send a Message

Materials: small sturdy mirrors
sunny day

Process:
1. Divide the class into partners or small groups.
2. *Challenge:* Send a message to your partner using a mirror and sunbeams.
3. Provide students with the time, space and materials to design a means to send messages.
4. Observe the groups sending messages to one another.

Try This:
- Try to crack the code and figure out the message being sent between other pairs.

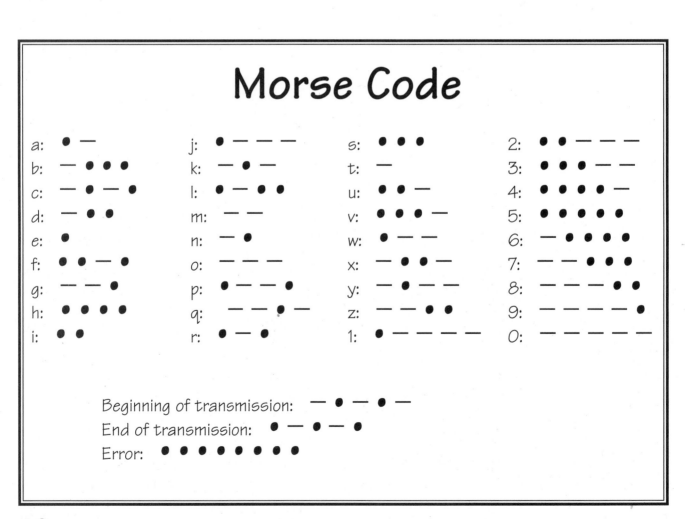

Morse Code

a: ● —	j: ● — — —	s: ● ● ●	2: ● ● — — —
b: — ● ● ●	k: — ● —	t: —	3: ● ● ● — —
c: — ● — ●	l: ● — ● ●	u: ● ● —	4: ● ● ● ● —
d: — ● ●	m: — —	v: ● ● ● —	5: ● ● ● ● ●
e: ●	n: — ●	w: ● — —	6: — ● ● ● ●
f: ● ● — ●	o: — — —	x: — ● ● —	7: — — ● ● ●
g: — — ●	p: ● — — ●	y: — ● — —	8: — — — ● ●
h: ● ● ● ●	q: — — ● —	z: — — ● ●	9: — — — — ●
i: ● ●	r: ● — ●	1: ● — — — —	0: — — — — —

Beginning of transmission: — ● — ● —
End of transmission: ● — ● — ●
Error: ● ● ● ● ● ● ● ●

Drum

K-3 🍪 ⏱ 🎁 ⚠Caution

The drum has been used in many cultures to send messages over distances, to tell stories or to express feeling.

Materials:
plastic container or tin can with one open end (tomato juice can works great)
1 large balloon

scissors
rubber band
small dowel, pencil or stick

Process:

1. Using scissors, cut the bottom off of the balloon.
2. Stretch the balloon tightly over the top of the tub or tin, if necessary put a rubber band around the rim to secure the balloon.
3. Use a tree twig, craft stick, piece of dowelling or pencil to beat on the drum.

Try This:

- Discuss the drum as an early form of long distance communication.
- To make the balloon easier to stretch, blow it up and let the air out prior to using it.
- Use different sized containers to create a whole drum set.
- Decorate the container with paints, stickers or wound cord prior to putting the balloon in place.
- Ask children to think about how the sound is made. How can the sound be altered?
- Encourage children to make and listen to a variety of sounds using their voices, their bodies and a variety of instruments and creative materials. Talk about the vibrations experienced, the pitch, the quality and the loudness of various sounds.
- Look around for scraps to make other instruments you can bang, scrape, tap, shake or blow.

* Caution: Be careful when using scissors.
* Caution: Do not put balloons in mouth.

Water Xylophone

 1-3 🍪 ⏱ ⚠ Caution

Materials:

8 small glass jars
water
food coloring (optional)
pouring container with spout (measuring cup, pitcher)
tapping device such as a small spoon, metal rod, knitting needle

Process:

1. Place the glass jars in a line.
2. Mix food coloring with water in a pouring container for visual effect.
3. Fill the first jar to the top with water.
4. Put a little less in the second jar, less again in the third and so on to the eighth jar.
5. Gently tap each jar and listen to the note it makes.

Try This:

- Ask children to describe how each of the sounds makes them feel.
- Does music communicate something? Look at music around the world and the messages and feelings it conveys.
- Incorporate this activity into your music curriculum. Study the xylophone, piano and other instruments.

* Caution: Be careful using glass jars.

Challenge:

Produce the musical scale using your water xylophone. If necessary, lead children to understand that removing and adding water will alter the sound. Can you play "Do-Re-Mi" or a simple tune?

String Phone

2-3

Children will discover that sound waves can travel along a material.

Materials:

2 clean, dry, empty tin cans with sealable lids removed (baby formula or coffee tins)

25 m fine string
bradawl and hammer

Process:

1. With assistance, have children punch a hole in the middle of the base of each can.
2. Push one end of the string into the bottom of one can and tie a large knot.
3. Fix the other end of the string into the second can in the same way.
4. Children form partners.
5. Take the telephone outdoors and ask one partner to walk away with one can until the string is pulled taut.
6. One child speaks into their can while the other listens into the open end of their can.
7. Children take turns sending messages back and forth to one another.
8. Help children to understand that their voice causes vibrations in the string. These vibrations travel along the string to the other can where they are picked up by a partner's ear.

Try This:

- Pluck the string. What kind of noise is made?
- Study the evolution of the telephone. Set up a display of early to recent telephones. Discuss how inventions have improved upon existing technology.
- Develop communication skills, by having students make phone calls.

* Caution: Be careful when making holes.

Challenge:

Improve the telephone! Design a telephone set that is better than the existing product.

Make a three-party string phone.

- *Alexander Graham Bell (1847-1922) worked with deaf people. His understanding of how the ear works led to his invention of a device that allowed speech to travel down a wire—that device was the telephone.*
- *In 1837 Samuel Morse invented the electric telegraph which sent messages by transmitting electrical pulses along a wire. His telegraph lines spanned the U.S. He then developed the famous Morse code, a system of dots and dashes, that allowed long and short electric signals to be translated into letters of the alphabet. His code has since been simplified but is still in use, especially in ship to shore communication. (See the Morse code on page 46.)*
- *Guglielmo Marconi, an Italian physicist and electrical engineer, invented the wireless telegraph, the radio and sent the first radio signal across the Atlantic in 1901.*

Design a Better Writing Contraption

 1-3

Materials: samples of various writing instruments (pens, pencils, chalk, char-
coal, markers, etc.)
paper
rubber bands

dowelling
straws
chalk
ink refill for ballpoint pens
thin markers

Process:
1. *Challenge:* Design a better writing contraption.
2. Provide children with the Challenge and the materials above.
3. Observe and assist where needed. Encourage students to think about shape, practicality, cost, convenience, appearance, shortcomings and limitations.

Try This:
- Investigate the various writing instruments down through the ages and around the modern world.
- Learn about Laszlo Biro (Ladislo Biro) (1900-1985) and the ballpoint pen, called the Biro in Europe. Biro invented the tiny metal ball tip for the pen and the ballpoint pen was invented. It was popular with British and American troops in WWII as it didn't leak with the changes in air pressure at high altitudes.
- Look at the invention of H.L. Lipmanh of Philadelphia, Pennsylvania. In 1858, he invented the popular pencil with a groove for rubber on the top.

Printing Press

2-3 1 10-60 min. *Caution

Materials:

potatoes
craft knife
paint
bowl
paper

Process:

1. Cut a potato in half.
2. Cut away part of the flat inside of the potato leaving a raised shape, letter or picture.
3. Pour paint onto a flat surface.
4. Press the flat of the potato into the paint.
5. Blot the painted surface once on a "blotter" paper.
6. Stamp the paper to be used, and your printing press is in business!

Try This:

- Using your printing press, make writing paper or wrapping paper.
- Study Johann Gutenberg (1397-1468) who pioneered printing with movable type or metal letters. In the early 1450s, he engraved mirror-image letters on blocks of metal, cast the letters in molds, cut them to shape and prepared them for printing. With the development of printing in Europe came thousands of books aiding the spread of ideas through the Western world from the fourteenth to sixteenth centuries. Gutenberg's method of printing stayed largely unchanged until the late twentieth century.

* Caution: Be careful when using the craft knife.

Challenge:

Devise a method to allow for continuous printing. Consider the use of a paint roller and small shapes or string.

Remote Control

1-3 SPACE

Materials:

remote control for television or
stereo
television or stereo which uses
remote control

various tin plates and pans
large space

Process:

1. *Challenge:* Using the remote control, turn on your television from another room.
2. Discuss how the remote control works. It sends an invisible, infrared modulated light signal from the hand unit through the air to the control panel.
3. Provide the materials and the Challenge. Allow children to experiment with various angles to bounce signals off of the pie plates and around corners.
4. Turn on the television or stereo from around the corner!

Try This:

• Discuss ways that this kind of technology could and does make life easier. (Emergency vehicles ability to control traffic lights, start your car from inside your house on a cold day, turn lights on or off from your bed, etc.)

Warning Alarm

K-3 10 min.

Materials:

tin cans
bells
string
Optional: materials
    for electrical circuit
    (see page 32)

Process:

1. *Challenge:* Design and construct a contraption that will announce the arrival of an intruder into your home, clubhouse, fort or classroom.
2. Provide materials and the Challenge and allow children to investigate, design, plan and produce their own unique alarm.

Try This:

• Discuss other uses for intruder warning contraptions.
• Add an electrical component to your alarm using the electrical circuit (see page 32).

Stethoscope

K-3 🧍 ⏱ 🛒

Listen to your heart!

Materials: 3 18" (45.72 cm) pieces of plastic or rubber tubing
glass Y tube
3 tiny metal funnels
3-ring binder or duotang
paper

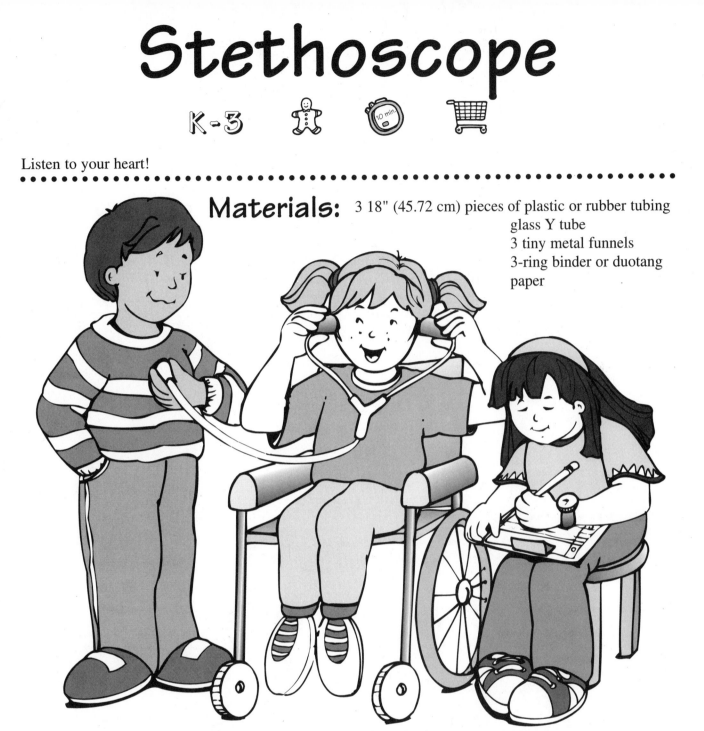

Process:
1. Attach one end of each piece of tubing to the ends of the glass Y tube.
2. Attach the funnels to the other ends of the tubing.
3. Hold two funnels over your ears and the third funnel on a friend's chest.
4. Listen for the heartbeat.

Try This:
- For a clearer heartbeat, place the funnel on bare skin directly over the heart.
- How many heartbeats can you hear per minute?
- How can you alter a person's heartbeat?

Chapter 6

Just for Fun
Contraptions, Toys and Other Neat Kid Stuff

The Great Toy Challenge

K-3

Materials:

Inventors' Kit
Creators' Corner
toy box of toys

Process:

1. Provide the Inventors' Kit and the Creators' Corner.
2. **Challenge:** Children are getting tired of the same old toys. Santa has asked you to design and build an exciting new toy. Can you help him? Can you invent a toy that has never been played with before?
3. Inspire children by providing a toy box of invented toys.
4. Facilitate learning with comments such as: "What a great idea! How can we make that? What could children do with that toy? How could we make this toy safe enough for young children?"
5. Present toys to one another and have a play session. Encourage discussion of the toys.

Try This:

- Make a display of the toys.
- Try to identify various types of machines evident within each toy.
- Set up a toy shop center. Allow children to design and build toys over a period of days or weeks.

- *Not all inventions help us with our work—some of the greatest inventions bring fun or entertainment to our lives.*
- *The jigsaw puzzle was invented by John Spilsbury to help his students learn geography. He glued a printed map of England and Wales to a piece of wood and then cut the map into pieces using a jigsaw.*

The Matching Contraption

 2-3

A great opportunity to turn knowledge into a game!

Materials:

sturdy cardboard
paper fasteners
2 3"-5" (7.62 x 12.7 cm) thin pieces dowelling
tape
wire
1.5 volt battery (AA, C or D cell)
1.5-3.0 volt flash-light battery
light bulb
bulb holder

Process:

1. Draw one column down the left and right side of the board.
2. Punch or mark a row with an equal number of holes down each column.
3. Attach a paper fastener in each hole.
4. In one column, draw one picture beside each paper fastener.
5. In the other column, print the word to identify each picture beside each fastener. Do not print the word in the position directly opposite the picture.
6. On the back of the cardboard, wrap the bare ends of the wire around the paper fasteners to connect each word to the corresponding picture.
7. Connect a wire from one terminal of the battery to one screw on the bulb holder.
8. Connect a long wire from the other screw on the light bulb holder to a dowel. Tape the wire to the dowel with a small section of wire exposed at the end of the dowel so it acts like a pointer or wand. Touch the dowels together to test the circuit.
9. Attach one end of the third wire to the battery terminal and the other end to the other dowel.
10. Touch one dowel to a paper fastener in one column, and the other dowel to a paper fastener in the other column. The appropriate picture to word match will allow the bulb to light up.

* Caution: Be careful using the battery.

Challenge:

Create a learn-to-read game or activity.

Reinforce math, reading, environmental studies, music theory or other knowledge with this matching contraption.

Have a Ball!

 K-3 🍪 ⏱

....

Materials:

rubber bands
aluminum foil
clothing scraps

old sock
needle and thread
samples of different types of balls

....

Process:

1. Explore the materials and the display of balls.

2. *Challenge:* You have forgotten to bring a ball on a picnic. All you have is this box of materials. Make a ball that children can play with.

3. Provide the materials, the Challenge and help children to crumple foil into a ball and wrap it in rubber bands for bounce; roll cloth and cover in rubber bands for bounce; stuff an old sock with rubber bands, cloth or foil and sew the ends. Praise inventive ideas.

4. Play catch, "basketball," wall ball, monkey in the middle or juggle.

....

Try This:

- Attach "tails" of various materials to the balls.
- Invent some new games to play with your kid-made balls. Teach the games to other children in the school yard. Host a Game Day.
- Study pioneer children and the kinds of balls they used.
- Learn about James Naismith, the Canadian who saw the need for an indoor team sport that combined excitement and skill. In 1891, he invented the game that came to be known as basketball!

Rock-a-Bye Baby

1-3 ⚠ Caution

Help the baby get back to sleep!

Materials:

berry basket or cardboard box
plastic pop bottle cut lengthwise
sturdy cardboard
balsa wood
craft wire for canopy
fabric for canopy and/or bedding
scissors

wire snips
craft knife
pencil
ruler or other measuring device
all-purpose glue, cool glue gun and
   glue sticks, wood glue
doll

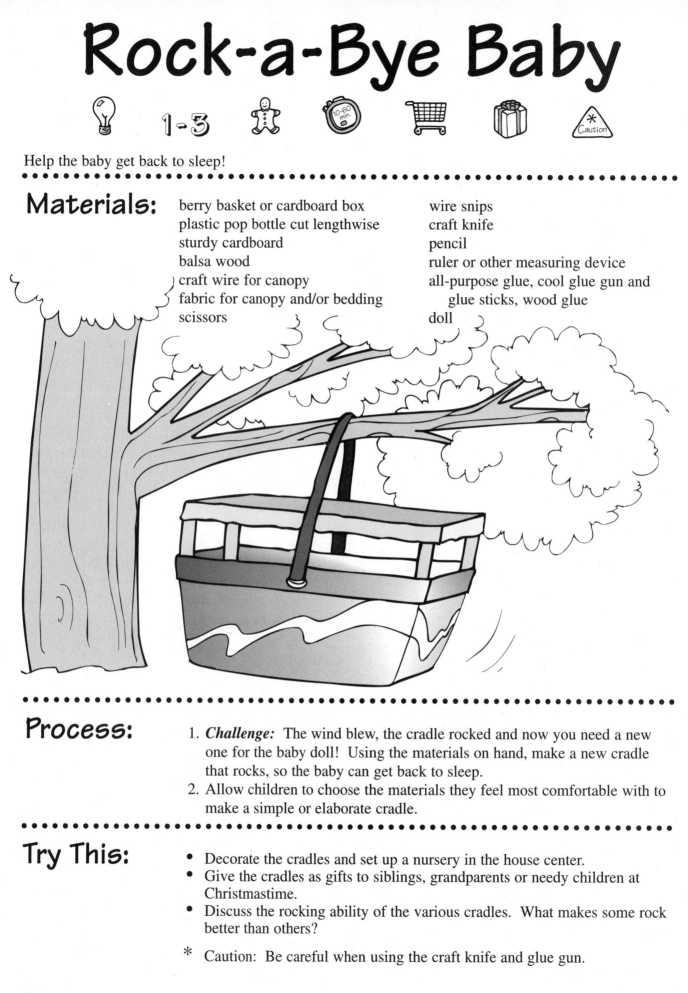

Process:

1. *Challenge:* The wind blew, the cradle rocked and now you need a new one for the baby doll! Using the materials on hand, make a new cradle that rocks, so the baby can get back to sleep.
2. Allow children to choose the materials they feel most comfortable with to make a simple or elaborate cradle.

Try This:

- Decorate the cradles and set up a nursery in the house center.
- Give the cradles as gifts to siblings, grandparents or needy children at Christmastime.
- Discuss the rocking ability of the various cradles. What makes some rock better than others?

* Caution: Be careful when using the craft knife and glue gun.

Balloon Power

   1-3

Materials:

long string
hook on wall
large sturdy straw or other tube

long, thin balloon
tape

Process:

1. Tie a long length of string to a hook on the wall or ceiling.
2. Pull the string taut and thread the straw onto the string.
3. Blow up the balloon, but do not tie it off.
4. Hold the neck of the balloon so that the air does not escape, and tape it to the straw with the neck of the inflated balloon facing away from the "destination."
5. Release the balloon and watch it go into space.
6. Discuss what happens as the balloon deflates. Why is the air expelled? What effect does it have? Talk about how the air is forced from the exhaust of a jet engine in much the same way, pushing the jet forward.

Try This:

• Discuss compression. If something is compressed or squished together by force, it will store energy that can be used later to propel something.

Challenge:

Can you reduce the friction between the straw and the string? Which works best, a taut string or a loose droopy string?

Reach Extender

K-3

Materials:
dowelling
glove
rubber band
soft stuffing (rags or quilting batting)

Process:
1. Stuff the glove with the filling material until it looks like a hand.
2. Attach the rubber band around the base of the glove.
3. Slip one end of the dowelling in the middle of the elastic.
4. Slide the elastic down over the glove and the dowelling to secure the glove in place.
5. Reach for things you couldn't get before.

Try This:
- Wave to your friends over a high fence or tap them on the shoulder from a distance.
- Dust the ceilings in your house.

Challenge:
Invent a method for moving the fingers of the glove.

Meals on Wheels

K-3

Materials:
10 to 15 marbles the same size   sturdy paper plate
Mason jar or other large lid   set of compasses
tape or glue

Process:
1. Use the compass to help you find the center of the plate, and mark the bottom of the plate.
2. Glue the jar lid onto the marked center.
3. Put marbles under the lid.
4. Put snacks or a dinner on the plate and pass it around!

Try This:
- See what happens when marbles are added or removed from the lid.

Challenge:
Invent a game using the rolling (or spinning) plate.

TLC10023 Copyright © Teaching & Learning Company, Carthage, IL 62321

Hand Torch

Materials:

take-apart flashlight
materials to make a circuit (see "Electricity Energy," page 32)

Inventors' Kit
Creators' Corner

Process:

1. Provide the opportunity for children to take a flashlight apart and investigate. Can they find the circuit?
2. ***Challenge:*** Design a flashlight that would be fun for a kid to use.
3. Provide the Challenge and materials and be ready with information or guidance.

Try This:

- Provide research materials that allow children to find out more about the first hand torch, later known as the flashlight. (Russian Conrad Hubert modified a friend's light-up flower invention to make a novelty electric hand torch that made him a millionaire!)

Clompers

1-3

Materials:

2 tin cans the same size
2 lengths of fine rope or sturdy string
    (approx. 5' [1.5 m] long)
hammer, bradawl (or nail) and wood block

Process:

1. Turn the tins upside down and mark a spot on either side of the tin just below the top ridge.
2. Using the wood block, hammer and nail, make holes on the marks.
3. Thread one rope through each can and tie the ends off.
4. Put your feet on top of the tins and hold the ropes–one in each hand.
5. Try clomping around!

Try This:

- Dance to music or play Follow the Leader while wearing your clompers.
- Recycle old jump ropes for the rope.
- Make your clomper footprints look like animal tracks by attaching modeling clay or other printmaking material.

* Caution: Be careful using the hammer and bradawl.

Challenge:

Clompers will slip on ice. Design a way to keep them from slipping.

Invent a way to attach them to your shoes so you won't have to hold the strings.

Someone is after you. Can you use your clompers to throw them off your track?

Water Wonder

1-3 · Caution

Make a contraption to take a message across the water.

Materials:

corks	balloon	tape
rubber bands	junior saw	note
balsa wood	plastic tubing	water table

Process:

1. **Challenge:** You live on one side of a small stream, and your friend lives on the other. You must get a note across the stream to your friend. Using the materials on hand, make a contraption that will take your note across for you.
2. Provide materials and the Challenge and observe and supervise as children develop their own contraptions.
3. Encourage students to think about powering their boat across the stream.
4. Test contraptions in the water table or small nearby stream.

Try This:

- Make watertight rafts to carry notes and the school address down a large body of water. Ask raft-finders to kindly respond to the note. Use pushpins to mark the journeys and locations of various rafts.

* Caution: Be careful using the junior saw.

Electricity in a Bottle

 K-3

Bring a contraption to life using static electricity!

Materials:

clear plastic 1 liter bottle with lid
cloth (silk or wool works best)
colored tissue paper or lightweight glittery confetti
paper punch–the kind that punches out neat shapes is best! (optional)

Process:

1. Cut or punch tiny confetti-sized shapes or characters in tissue paper.
2. Pour the paper bits into the plastic container and close the lid.
3. Rub the plastic surface with the cloth. Watch the bits inside pop around as the surface gets charged with static electricity.

Try This:

- Listen.
- Remove the lid and hold the bottle upside down. Why don't the bits fall out?
- Try other things inside the bottle, like salt or sugar. Can you get them to dance?
- Rub a balloon's surface on fabric or your head until it is charged. Attach a paper nose, eyes, mouth and some crazy hair.

Challenge:

Your best friend is ill and must stay in bed for a long time. Design a "toy-in-a-bottle" that would be easy to play with in bed.

Resources

Evaluating a Child's Creative Thinking Progress

• •

To evaluate creative thinking, observe the child in a wide variety of activities. Focus on growth, the process of problem solving and imaginative thinking. Assess a broad base of concept and skill development using observation checklists, anecdotal comments, achievement records, creative outcomes, growth profiles and portfolios. Photographic records of contraptions make an excellent ongoing record of progress and provide a base for discussion and evaluation. Children from three to nine years of age will participate with natural enthusiasm and curiosity. They demonstrate sustained interest in creating and problem solving. Through hands-on experience they will use their senses to explore and discriminate, ask questions and express ideas freely and develop increasing language, cognitive, social and motor abilities. Watch for these particular skills.

• •

Child three to five years of age will:

- use a trial and error method to explore physical properties of objects
- make simple casual relationships by association
- demonstrate intuitive feel for symmetry, scale and order
- manipulate materials in inventive ways
- use tools in an individual manner limited by fine and gross motor skill development
- become visually aware of detail
- experiment with form, space and movement

• •

Child five to seven years of age will:

- demonstrate an understanding of cause and effect
- follow three-step instructions
- manipulate materials in inventive ways
- recognize similarities and differences
- develop visual awareness of shape, detail, scale, design, conservation and symmetry
- begin to make plans before carrying out an activity
- see parts or wholes but not parts in relation to wholes
- recognize symbolic forms
- demonstrate a variety of problem-solving techniques

• •

Child seven to nine years of age will:

- demonstrate a good understanding of cause and effect
- focus on detail without losing sight of the whole
- conserve number and length
- express and receive ideas in symbolic forms
- manipulate materials in creative ways
- make use of a rich vocabulary before, during and after an activity
- manipulate tools and materials in a competent manner
- demonstrate an understanding of scale, balance, design, space detail and motion
- preplan work through discussion and sketches

Evaluation of the Child

You may wish to use this checklist several times per child during the year. Date your evaluation so you can compare and note areas of progress.

Child's name _____ Date _____ Does the child . . .	Never	Some-times	Always
Recognize a need that could be addressed with design and technology?			
Demonstrate initiative?			
Experiment and manipulate materials in an inventive manner?			
Use vocabulary that indicates an understanding of science and technology?			
Demonstrate the ability to organize and plan a project appropriate for age level?			
Show attention to materials, detail, practicality and scientific principle?			
Demonstrate a working knowledge of the tools needed to create?			
Make use of a variety of techniques to create and complete works?			
Demonstrate a degree of visual awareness appropriate to his age level?			
Demonstrate an increasing awareness of detail, scale, conservation, symmetry and use of space?			
Express ideas about the work verbally?			
Demonstrate insight into various activities?			
Incorporate creative thinking and problem-solving skills when creating a work?			
Demonstrate progressive skill development?			
Consolidate problem-solving skills in all areas?			
Demonstrate an understanding of the end product created?			
Work well in group projects?			
Appraise own work?			
Take pride in his work?			
Show an appreciation of classmates' efforts and differences?			
Complete given tasks?			
Demonstrate a sustained interest and enthusiasm in activities?			

Scavenger Lists

Where Can I Find Free Materials?

Seek out the best spots in your area to scavenge great materials. Send a letter home with students that lists the kinds of materials your classroom could use, and you will tap into a valuable resource. Enlist the help of local businesses, express an interest in excess materials, samples, donations or some valuable trash.

hardware store
art supply store
local newspaper office
framing shop
electronics shop
small equipment repair shop
recycling center
woodworking shop
building site
auto repair shop
garden center
thrift shop
fast food restaurant
grocery store
textiles company

office supply store
computer shop
craft supply store
floral shop
electrician's business
waste management facility
lumberyard
old toolboxes
students' homes and attics
clothing manufacturer
garage sales
airline company
moving company
flooring company

Try This:

- Provide shopkeepers and business owners with a large box that has your name on it, and ask them to save interesting scraps for you. Pick up your box once a month.
- *Where do you keep all this junk?* Make storage easier by sorting materials into boxes. Materials should be readily visible and attainable by students.
- Cut, shape, fold, crumple or combine particular materials to stimulate inventive thoughts.
- If you can't find what you need, make it.

Materials Worth Scavenging

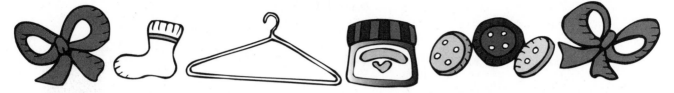

ball bearings
magnets
clock workings
metal ruler
specialized glues
small vise
computer chips
discarded computer equipment
discarded appliances and utensils
discarded toys
various kinds of tape
balsa wood
large and small buttons
corks
metal washers
clothespins
beads and beans
wire
ribbons and shoelaces
rubber scraps
jar seals
reusable containers
pipe cleaners
craft sticks
cartons and boxes of all
   shapes and sizes
Plasticine™ and clays
paper clips and fasteners
polystyrene packing peanuts
   and trays
tin trays, pans and cans
coat hangers
carpets and flooring scraps
thread spools
plastic bottles

wheels from toys, skates, bicycles
plastic tubing
broom handles and dowels
discarded tools
kitchen cutting board
computer disks
segments of rubber hose
electronic components
old telephones
old jewelry
old running shoes
wood scraps
fabric scraps with interesting
   textures
toothpicks and skewer sticks
screw hooks and eyes
paintbrushes
coins and keys
string, yarn, twine and thread,
   waxed floss
sealable plastic bags
wallpaper sample books
balloons
rubber bands and elastic string
frame shop mat scraps
cardboard
paper rolls and cups
foam balls
safety pins
bubble wrap
foil wrap
straws
edibles: marshmallows, gumdrops
thumbtacks
matchboxes

Basic Skills for
Making Working Models

Planning

How do you turn an idea into a working model? Help children explore this question. Provide opportunities for children to plan, discuss, assess materials and equipment available, sketch and measure, make a design plan, make lists and invite assistants.

Measuring: Provide instruction and equipment for measuring and marking before making holes, shaping or cutting.
Measure twice; cut once!

Using Tools and Equipment

An important part of turning ideas into contraptions is learning to plan and use tools and materials properly. Safety guidelines should be made clear to children. Caution and supervision is required when using all tools.

Cutting and Shaping Using Sharp Tools

Sharp tools are dangerous! Supervision is essential!

Scissors: Scissors should be used for cutting cardboard, paper and other light materials. They are the safest cutting tool. Keep closed when not in use; work with the tips facing away from the body. Adult supervision may be required for the cutting of heavy materials.

Knives: Kitchen knives will work for some projects. A sharp craft knife may be used for cutting soft wood. Cut one section at a time, with a smooth, steady motion, blade facing away from you, on a flat, firm surface. Straight lines can be cut against a metal ruler. Always keep fingers away from the blade.

Junior Saw: A junior saw can be used for cutting materials that cannot be cut by scissors. Adult supervision is essential. Mark the cutline with pencil. Put the material to be cut in a small table vise, C-clamp or bench hook, or have it held firmly in place. Use a flat, sturdy work surface.

Joining and Connecting

A **spirit level** will show you if the materials are joined straight and level.

Glues: Glues join most material easily. White glue or carpenter's glue will work for most projects. Avoid glues containing cyanoacrylate, fungicides or those with harmful vapors.

Cool Glue Gun: A cool glue gun with glue sticks will provide a fast, sturdy bond. Despite its name, this glue gun is still hot enough to cause a burn, and adult supervision should be provided. Caution should be taken not to touch the glue or the gun until cool.

Connecting: Paper, cardboard and fabric can be joined with paper fasteners, staples, tape, tacks or Velcro™.

Needle and Thread: Supervision should be provided. A needle threader will be helpful.

Hammering: Large sturdy pieces of wood can be nailed together. Use junior hammers and ensure that the heads are firmly attached to the shafts. For safe hammering, push the nail into a scrap cardboard holder, and hold the cardboard while hammering the nail or predrill the hole with a very small drill bit.

Making Holes

Holes should be marked before punching or drilling.

Punch: A single-hole paper or leather punch will work well on many light-weight materials, paper, leather, fabric, cardboard and some plastics.

Bradawl, Center Punch or Knitting Needle: Mark the position and poke the hole. Work over a thick piece of polystyrene, soft scraps of wood or cutting board to prevent injury and damage to surfaces. Use different thickness for different size holes.

Hand Drill: Holes may be started with the bradawl or knitting needle or center punch before drilling. Drill on a flat, soft, surface such as a layer of polystyrene or similar material. Materials to be drilled can be held in a vise or C-clamp. Tie back long hair, necklaces or other materials that could get caught in the drill; replace blunt drill bits; supply goggles if children will be near the drilling action and keep fingers away from exposed gears.

Finishing

Smoothing: A surface can be smoothed or sharp edges rounded with a file or sandpaper. A sanding block will make sanding flat surfaces quick and easy. Wrap a block of wood with sandpaper and fastened paper edges on the back. Inexpensive commercially made blocks can be obtained from hardware or building stores.

Covering with Paint, Stains and Varnishes: Apply paint with a brush, stain with a wide brush or cloth and varnish with a wide brush. Read contents of container carefully. Wear old clothing as it will surely get a spot somewhere.

Encourage respect and proper care for all tools and equipment.

The Great Invention Convention

Host an Invention Convention to encourage creative ideas and to provide a forum for sharing inventions.

Display Categories
Inventions that make life easier.
Inventions that make life better.
Inventions that make life more fun.

Set up your Invention Convention as a competition or a cooperative sharing of inventive ideas. Display the inventions in the gymnasium or library.

Prepare for the Convention
Lead up to your event with a study of important inventions, a look at famous inventors and a visit from a local inventor.

Share the Excitement!
Invite parents, friends, members of local businesses, students from other schools, politicians and other community members who will recognize students' achievements.

Get Coverage
Invite the local media to cover your event.

Invention Station
Have one group of students research and present information on some well-known inventions. Participants may visit this station to learn about popular inventions.

Name That Invention
Set up a table with obscure inventions. Participants guess what they think each item might be. Record answers and provide a prize for a student who names all of the items.

Meet Benjamin Franklin
One group of children is designated to role-play. Each child is assigned an inventor to study and take on the character of. These inventors mingle throughout the convention, answering questions about their lives and inventions.

Provide Convention Challenges
The Box Challenge: Turn a box inside out. Provide boxes, scissors and tape or glue.
Take Apart Challenge: Take an object apart. Provide screwdrivers; pliers; tweezers; a variety of take-apart items such as clocks, motors, radios, cassette players . . . .
Design a Better Playground: Make a model of a better playground. Provide straws, toothpicks, skewers, discs, wooden shapes, plasticine, marshmallows, string, and tape.

Bibliography

Ardley, Neil. *Dictionary of Science*. Dorling Kindersley Limited, Raincoast Books, Vancouver, 1994.

Bender, Lionel. *Invention*. Eyewitness Books, Dorling Kindersley Limited, Stoddart Publishing Co., Canada, 1991. Also available in U.S. through Houghton Mifflin Company, Boston.

Carletti, Silvana, Suzanne Girard, and Kathlene Willing. *Sign Out Science: Simple Hands-On Experiments Using Everyday Materials*. Markham, ON: Pembroke Publishers Ltd., 1993.

Carpenter, Thomas. *Inventors: Profiles in Canadian Genius*. Camden House Publishing/Telemedia Publishing Inc./Firefly Books, 250 Sparks Avenue, Willowdale, Canada, 1990.

Clements, Gillian. *The Picture History of Great Inventors*. Alfred A. Knopf, New York, 1994.

Kydd, G., and Ricki Wortzman. *Explorations in Science*. Addison Wesley, 1992.

Lowery, Lawrence. *The Everyday Science Sourcebook: Ideas for Teaching in the Elementary and Middle School*. University of California, Berkeley, Dale Seymour Publications, 1985.

Macaualay, David. *The Way Things Work*. Houghton Mifflin Company, Boston, 1988.

Newton, Doug and Lynn. *Design and Technology* (Bright Ideas Series). Scholastic, 1990.

Norris, Doreen, and Joyce Boucher. *Observing Children in the Formative Years*. The Board of Education for the City of Toronto, Toronto, 1989.

Richards, R. *An Early Start to Technology*. Simon & Schuster, Toronto, 1990.

Richardson, Robert. *The Weird and Wondrous World of Patents*. Sterling Publishing Co., Inc., New York, 1990.

Willing, K.R., and S. Girard. *Learning Together: Computer-Integrated Classrooms*. Markham, ON: Pembroke Publishers Ltd., 1990.

Wyatt, Valerie. *Inventions: An Amazing Investigation*. Owl Books/Greey de Pencier Books, Toronto, 1987.